Otters

James Maclaine

Illustrated by Maribel Lechuga

Additional illustrations by Bonnie Pang

Designed by Tom Ashton-Booth and Helen Edmonds

Otter consultant: Professor David Macdonald CBE,
Wildlife Conservation Research Unit, Zoology Department, University of Oxford

Reading consultant: Alison Kelly

Contents

Types of otters

There are 13 different types of otters. They all have long tails, little ears and short legs.

This is a Eurasian otter.

It has very long whiskers on its face.

Where otters live

Otters live in water and on land. They can be found near rivers, streams, lakes, ponds, swamps and on seashores.

Sea otters live in very cold places where the sea often freezes.

They spend almost all their lives in water.

Most types of otters mark places to show where they live.

An otter rubs smells from its body onto logs, plants and rocks.

It also leaves piles of smelly dung. Otter dung is known as spraint.

When another otter sniffs these smells, it finds out that an otter is living nearby.

Hideaways

Most otters hide and rest in places known as dens or holts.

Some otters dig holes in river banks to make their dens.

Marine otters hide in small caves beside the sea.

African clawless otters use their dens to stay cool when it's very hot outside.

Some otters make their dens warm by lining them with plants.

This otter is collecting grass to carry back to its den.

Super swimmers

Otters are excellent at swimming.

They use their strong, short legs to paddle along the surface.

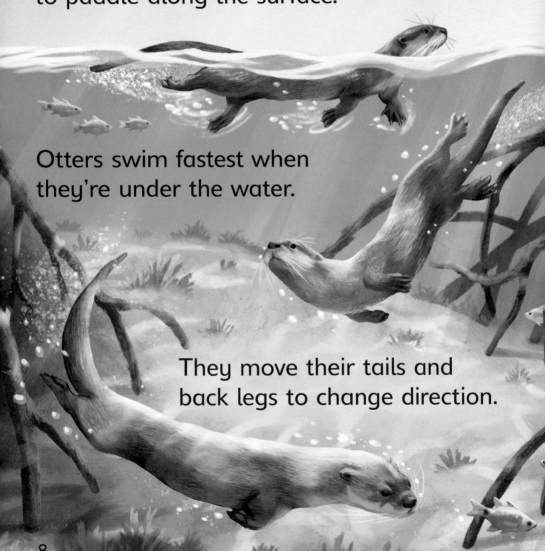

Otters swim fastest when they're under the water.

They move their tails and back legs to change direction.

After swimming, an otter's fur looks spiky.
Water drips off easily, so the fur dries quickly.

When otters dive,
they close their ears
and noses to keep
out water.

They can see
underwater, so they
keep their eyes open.

Moving on land

Otters move in different ways when they're on land.

This Eurasian otter is running in the snow.

Lots of otters use their strong paws to climb across rocks.

They also lie on their tummies to slide down slopes.

Eurasian otters
can move fast
even when it's icy.

Some otters roll on
the ground. This
helps to dry their fur.

Sea otters sometimes
rest on land. They
waddle quite slowly.

How otters hunt

Some otters hunt during the day.
Others hunt at night.

This North American river otter is using
its teeth and paws to catch a fish.

Sea otters carry food
they catch so they
can keep hunting.

Otters hunt fish in different ways.

A spotted-necked otter spots a fish from the surface, then dives to catch it.

A hairy-nosed otter traps fish in tree roots that grow in water.

Smooth-coated otters swim together in a V-shape so fish can't easily escape.

Hungry otters

As well as fish, otters eat frogs, mice, insects, small birds and different types of sea creatures.

A sea otter floats on its back after catching an octopus.

It holds the octopus on its chest and eats part of it at a time.

When it has finished, the otter rolls over to wash its fur.

Otters have strong, sharp teeth that are good for chewing and crunching.

This otter is crushing a crab's shell, so it can eat the soft parts inside.

If a sea otter eats lots of sea urchins, its teeth turn purple.

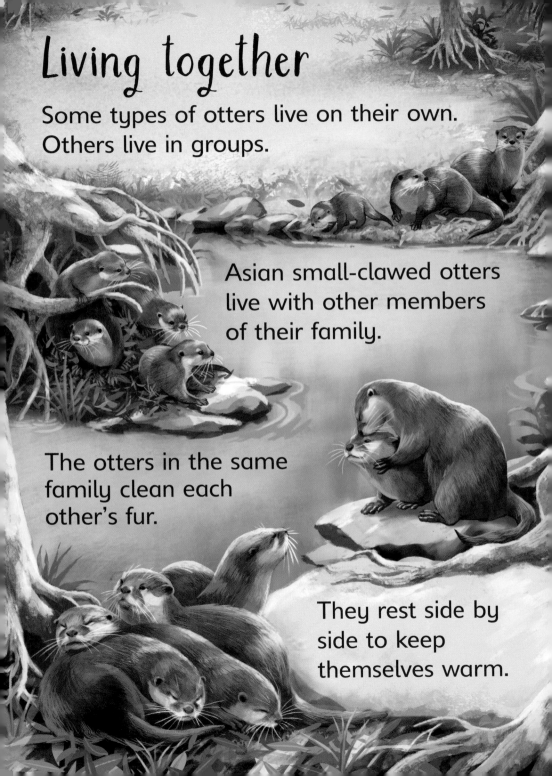

Living together

Some types of otters live on their own.
Others live in groups.

Asian small-clawed otters
live with other members
of their family.

The otters in the same
family clean each
other's fur.

They rest side by
side to keep
themselves warm.

Some otters work together to stay safe.

The smooth-coated otters in a group spot a crocodile near where they live.

The otters chase the crocodile and try to bite its tail.

They keep chasing the crocodile until it swims away.

Baby otters

Mother otters have up to six babies at a time. The babies are known as pups.

Most pups are born inside a den. They already have fur, but they cannot see.

The pups drink their mother's milk every few hours.

After five weeks, they start to open their eyes.

If a mother otter needs to move one of her pups, she picks it up gently with her mouth.

Baby sea otters are born at sea.
Their mothers carry them on their chests.

This pup is only
six days old.

Growing up

Young otters have lots to learn as they grow up.

These North American river otter pups have left their den. They're exploring the edge of the lake where they live.

Most pups start to swim when they're a few months old. Their mother teaches them.

Otter pups learn how to fight and hunt as they play with each other.

Some young otters follow the adults in their group and copy what they do.

Sea otter pups learn quickly. They can dive when they're just six weeks old.

Noisy otters

Otters make lots of different noises.

A mother otter whistles at her pups to tell them to follow her.

African clawless otters bark if they spot an animal that's dangerous.

The giant otters in a group hum to each other to show that they're nearby.

Otters are very noisy when they fight. They grunt, snarl and hiss to scare each other.

These Eurasian otters are fighting in a river.

Otter fur

Otters have lots and lots of short hairs on their bodies that trap air and keep them warm.

They also have a waterproof layer of long, oily hairs. This keeps them dry.

This sea otter is fluffing up its fur with its paws.

Otters clean their fur because dirt and salt make it less waterproof.

Salt is left on a Eurasian otter's fur when it swims in salty seawater.

The otter finds fresh water in a stream and washes the salt from its fur.

Otters also chew their fur to clean it. They can reach the fur all over their bodies.

Paws and claws

Otters have five toes on each of their paws. Some otters have claws, too.

Look closely at this giant otter's paws. Can you see webs of skin between the toes?

Its webbed paws are good for swimming.

Otters use their paws in different ways.

African clawless otters lift up stones to find things to eat.

Congo clawless otters dig in mud to search for worms.

Neotropical otters use their claws to help them climb along branches.

Clever otters

Otters use different tricks when they're trying to find food or rest.

Otters can hunt in muddy water because their whiskers sense when fish move.

Asian small-clawed otters put mussels in a sunny spot to make their shells open up.

Some sea otters hammer sea snails against rocks to smash their shells.

This sea otter is asleep. It has wrapped itself in a type of seaweed called kelp.

The kelp stops it from drifting away.

Sleeping sea otters sometimes hold paws so they don't drift apart.

Glossary

Here are some of the words in this book you might not know. This page tells you what they mean.

 whisker - a long, stiff hair. Otters have whiskers on their faces.

 spraint - otter dung. Most otters mark where they live with spraint.

 den - a place where some animals rest. Otter dens are also called holts.

 pup - a baby otter. It takes about a year for most pups to grow up.

 claw - a sharp nail. Many otters have five claws on each paw.

 webbed - a type of paw that has thin skin between the toes.

 kelp - a type of seaweed. Sea otters live where there's lots of kelp.

Usborne Quicklinks

Would you like to find out more about otters?
You can visit Usborne Quicklinks for links to websites
with videos, amazing facts and things to make and do.

Go to **usborne.com/Quicklinks** and type in
the keywords "**beginners otters**".
Make sure you ask a grown-up before going online.

Notes for grown-ups

Please read the internet safety guidelines at Usborne Quicklinks
with your child. Children should be supervised online. The websites
are regularly reviewed and the links at Usborne Quicklinks are
updated. However, Usborne Publishing is not responsible and does
not accept liability for the content or availability of any website
other than its own.

These sea otters are resting together on some floating ice.